The Man who brought Copper and Gold

Susi Clare

ISBN: 978-93-88319-59-1

First Edition: 2021
Rs. 200/-

Cyberwit.net
HIG 45 Kaushambi Kunj, Kalindipuram
Allahabad - 211011 (U.P.) India
http://www.cyberwit.net
Tel: +(91) 9415091004
E-mail: info@cyberwit.net

Printed at Thomson Press India Limited.

Dedication

To my friends, for love, laughter and … dog-sitting.

Acknowledgements and Thanks

Some of these poems, or earlier versions, have appeared in anthologies published by Weyfarers, Seafield Publishing, I Cento Castelli, Poetry on the Lake; in Orbis; on line at Hungry Hill Poetry and Poets Meet Painters, the Poets in Residence blog, and at Poetry *pf*.

Special thanks to Christopher North and Anne Stewart for their invaluable generosity and encouragement; to Robert Morley for his much-appreciated help; to Gabriella Ripepi for her wonderful cover design; to Karen Howells and Tracey Radaelli for beautiful friendship and support, technological and other.

Contents

AIDE-MEMOIRE

Are you sitting comfortably? asks Mother, as if she's
Daphne Oxenford back in the Fifties and you're
sitting on a sofa instead of a wooden chair
that's making your thighs go numb.
There's an art to cleaning silver, she begins, letting
the tang of Duraglit flare like moths' wings.
You strum a bead border with a toothbrush,
deaf-ear the glossary she recites on automatic replay -
you've heard it all before.
More elbow-grease, she says, *it won't clean itself.*
You frown at her arms, plump as rolled chicken,
strong enough to land a calf, at your own puny
limbs, good for nothing but a scolding.
You're breathless from fumes and the longing
to be in your room, playing with a pink plastic
tea set, pretend cakes, pretending to be grown up.

Now you are, and occasionally, in odd outdoor places,
you feel a sting in your nose, sharp, acrid;
inside your mind, her litany:
acanthus, acorn, curlicue - floriate, foliate, finial -
scallops, scrolls, swags - and the one you'd roll
your tongue around - *repoussé gadroon.*

BUTTER AND MY FATHER

My Father left me an unfamiliar self.
Back then, I cursed him to kingdom come; I wanted
the father-daughter thing like the ringleted child
attached to him in photos, the cosy, fatty-acid
snacks before bed, growing up.
I still have the questions I couldn't ask
and he wouldn't have answered, like, for instance,
what he did in the Arab desert, since surely
there was more to his war than the eco-friendly
operations of dung beetles;
why he gave up singing;
why he kissed that tart at someone's Christmas party;
why he did what he did.

Wherever he is, heaven or some place in between,
we can't negotiate with words.
So, for starters, I want to give up talking to him
as if he might re-appear. I want to enjoy
small pleasures, enjoy how,
when I'm peckish after a night out and take
the Lurpak from the fridge, I remember
that him, back from the pub, bricklaying butter
onto slabs of bread; how
he leaned on the mantelpiece, casting the cast
in his eye on me, his grin that said *More for me!*
knowing I'd take a slice; and always
mother sarkily asking if he liked bread with his butter,
and him looking as if it wouldn't melt in his mouth.

SHED

A certain look would shut my Granddad's face
as surely as a steel door;
I was ten and watched it all, recognised signs,
tactics, kept out of cross-fire,
never missed a trick.
We'd sit across the hearth in a snood
of beef and cabbage, while Grandma, ramrod
at the washing-up, sent messages
in code in bubbles of Fairy.
I'd wait for his eyes to breach the span
of soccer scores, the taste of a wink so slight
it might have been a one-eyed blink.
It came, and as it went, he tuned us out,
face emptied like a glass of milk,
the only vital signs smoke from the Woodbine
cindering between his teeth,
his quivering squint.
On the dot of two o'clock, she cracked
the tea-towel and he'd rise,
the imprint of his rump slowly leavening
to give the cushion back its face,
her sigh and Woman's Hour shooing
him down the path to his garden shed.
I'd hang around the door, scuffing toe-caps,
toying with splinters on the jamb, reassured
by the acid tang in my mouth of shaven wood,
red-eyed bubbling metal,
not helping, not getting in the way,
none the wiser.

PATCH

They wouldn't let me take Patch with me
after they'd coaxed me from my hiding-place
with the nonsense bribes made to children

laying hands hard on my shoulders to tug me
like uprooting a sapling, saying
it's all right, your Mum's home, you can see her now

dragging my feet through a syrup of dread
staring at the fat-burnt being they called my mother
mask of ointment thick as Sunday dripping

and the grease splitting, bubbling promises
my face creasing to peach stone
heart sledging at my chest

and not speaking even if I'd wanted to, even
if I'd managed to push words
through the caved-in hole of my throat

slipping like wet soap from those clutching fingers
fear steam-rolling my wits
desperate to hold the cuddly and familiar

diving onto my bed, into his fluffy embrace
pressing tears into the acrylic comfort of his fur
making myself deaf, making myself not see.

COAL HOLE

It was a scorcher that summer
of shorts and cropped tops,
breasts that happened overnight,
boys with different games in mind,
dogging us as we wandered on the rec,
herding us towards the copse,
muscled with hormones,
slit-eyed with purpose.

After that, we took Granddad's dog.
They shrugged away, all but two, lust-struck
from top-shelf magazines, saliva
hissing through teeth, the reek
of teenage civet hitting us in the face.
Then, *See 'em off, Lassie*, you said,
and she barked, twice, snarled
as they weevilled closer, snapped at air.

Next day, a clatter of sling-backs
in the yard, two mothers, tough as anvils,
bouffants and cross-your-heart bras,
unwrapping grievances on the kitchen step,
voices like synthetic strawberries.
And you, vibrating with outrage, so sure
Granddad would take your side,
village applecart be damned.
Instead, he hauled Lassie off to the coal hole,
left her there all night.
Later, you said it felt like something ripping inside,

too torn to mend.
Quietly, you took him off his pedestal,
shut him in a dark place too.

GRANDDAD'S SNAP TIN

Stencilled with posies now and home to photos, brought down
from a shelf too high for us to reach on rainy summer afternoons
as Grandma toasted crumpets on the fire.
Dominos on the rug, freckled with melting butter.
Sepia snaps and black-and-whites. Stories.

This: a Father and Son bowling along a prom in a bustle
of Fifties' turn-ups; in tow, a Mother, a Daughter-in-law,
belly huge as if she'd swallowed the sun, skewered smiles,
legs lifted like showgirls in mid-kick.

This: a Grandfather, slicked and spruced, showing off
his boxing medals, teeth shy, feisty only in his fists;
held a shiny Davy lamp away as if he didn't know it was
the brass handshake from the colliery, seams of coal in his lungs.

This: a Grandmother, whalebone-slim by the caravan,
skirt billowing like a Marilyn pin-up, mouth open to the sky;
dwarfed by old age and loneliness, seduced by Valium
and rum in her morning tea, no match for the lorry.

This: a Father, trim as a gun, building castles with his kids
in sand far removed from the desert of North Africa;
arm grafted to his stomach in a sling of his own skin, blood clot
biding its time, waiting for a Thomson flight to Madeira.

This: a Mother, squishy as Turkish Delight in a deck chair,
tears making her new-born's face run watery into the blue;

helpless as her husband died in a foreign bed; lived with blackness
and bitters for twenty years, until her second chance.

This: a Son, sausage-roll forelock ravelling, wide-kneeing
the sea, yelping as waves turned on him and caught his tail;
whittled acrimony and divorce into fury and hate,
became a man who spoke with his hands.

This: a Daughter, smocked pink cozzie, scowling
for the birdie, foam pirating pebbles from under her toes;
escaped to a different world, left the old behind,
never looked back, never went back.

An esplanade, grey pleat of North Sea, a caravan site, a beach;
on the back, shaky purpled writing: *Skegness, 1956.*

CLACTON 1967

First thing he says, *You dolled up for Carnival or what?*
Does he mean my Twiggy eyes, or the pink spray-on highlight?
Whichever, my face feels like a smacked bum and something's
doing a bungee jump in my stomach.
OK, so he *is* a bit of rough and my mum'd have kittens
if she knew what I was up to, but there's the thrill, that
and his blue eyes, black hair, pale face, which, let's face it,
is kind of rat-like in daylight but nicely chiselled by night.
Plus he doesn't go to my school.
He slides his tongue over the Rizla, studies me through smoke
as if I'm a prize heifer. The pinkie nail he files to a point slices
along the streak in my hair, flicks it away, like dandruff.
He hefts the front of his drainpipes, grinds the dog-end
with a fake-snake winklepicker, says, *Oh well, come on then*,
and sets off down the alley, not waiting to see if I follow.
He pushes me against the wall of the Variety Hall; I feel
the pulse of band music through bricks on my back, his pulse
on my stomach; I'm encased in throbbing.
His tongue laps my ear, delves, twirls;
when he takes it out, the skin turns cold.
He moves to my lips, they part without thinking twice;
I taste the bitterness of wax.
Let's get these buns out of the bag, he says to my teeth;
bra wire digs into my ribs.
His fingers zipper the bulge at the top of my nylons;
Time to put the roger back in rabbit, he says, fiddling with his flies.
I'm thinking, *rabbit? What rabbit?* Then twig.
I'm not that kind of girl, I say, clamping my knees
tight enough to crush an Aspirin.

You're a bleedin' tease is what you are.
He spits the words at me. For a minute I quail, but he pulls out
a comb, tweaks his Elvis quiff; the Zippo flares behind his palm.
See you around then, he says.
It starts raining; pink leaks down my face
like the bloody tears of a plaster saint.
By the time he reaches the corner, he's shrunk
into perspective. In the lamp-light, he squares
his shoulders under the baggy red blazer, making ripples
in the logo, almost turning the final exclamation
into a question mark.

FACE AT THE WINDOW

There's not much pleasure left in life,
is what she says, chafing bony fingers
as if she's trying to light sticks.
She's parked in the wheelchair that sleeps
in a corner, so close to the window
her hair looks part of the curtain,
caught in tiny nooses of lace.
You can still enjoy your garden.
It's a ploy to chivvy her and she knows it,
puckering her lips and rubbing at chinks
of sunlight on the blanket kilting her knees.
She leans sideways, straining to right a hem;
even that's too much for her now.
Let's get some fresh air. I'll push.

Red Admirals snuffle in the buddleia, dragonflies
dither on the pond, debating who to mate.
What a racket, she says with a smile as we pass
sparrows housekeeping in the holly tree.
We both ignore the cottage behind us;
we know the room is waiting patiently
as a family retainer to welcome her back,
waiting behind broderie anglaise to smother
her in its smells and silence and claustrophobia;
until the day she won't go back at all.

THE DAY WE CLEARED OUT GRANDMA'S HOUSE

Mother jams the door open with half a wooden peg;
old air moves, a bluebottle fizzes.
I step into my own fairy-tale – the kitchen I knew has shrunk.
It's a wonder they managed, new wife and mother-in-law,
skirting each other like Spanish dancers. Or duellists.
Two years of hell, says Mother. *Your Father never stood up to her.*

No one's been here since the accident; there are things in the fridge
that don't belong; on the table, a half-Hovis keeping secrets,
milk, blissfully mephitic, a trinity of china tea cup, leaves unread,
bottle of Valium, cut-price rum.
G.P.'s Band-Aid, says Mother, *and Grandma's little helper*;

an undertow at the back of mirrors, memories stored in glass:
crab sandwiches and beetle drives; mince pies and Advocaat and darts;
custard creams and Ovaltine; Yardley's and question-mark skirts;
almost-whiffs of washdays and bluing, coal dust,
Granddad's Navy Cut, her Coty L'Aimant – or was it Je Reviens?
Neither, says Mother. *She wore 4711*;

twin armchairs, exactly where they've always been, turning to
one another. Smudged bifocals. *Haa, haa*, she'd breathe
on each lens, rubbing furiously with her pinny, feet up on a stool.
On the rug, Cornish romance, autumn pages closed in on themselves.
That's a turn-up, says Mother. *She only used to read Woman's Own;*

a library of hoarded fashions in drawers, wardrobes.
And Faith, Hope and Charity, speckled with milk-chocolate mist,
glaring from ovals of darkness tunnelled into the wall.
Grandma used to say they were paintings of Irish ancestors.
In her dreams, says Mother, bubble-wrapping the chamber pot.
She was illegitimate, adopted at birth.

WISH YOU WERE HERE

beside me on this bay of scumbled rocks,
silence so heavy it's almost edible,
lake breathing itself gently onto the shore,
a cob and pen, wings arched, pedalling water, looping
round to meet in a heart of breast and beak.

It's a tryst, a vow, with San Carlo's silent blessing
(how you hated the climb up his innards that day,
walls pressing in, shrinking you);
then only the swans, eurhythmic, sailing
in mist towards me, like beacons.

THE UNDERSTORY

Close your eyes and open your hand, he says, hulling
a neat, glossy chestnut from its clitter of quills.
She strokes its hard roundness; whorls escape
as she lifts her thumb to circle back.

Close your eyes and listen, he says. Not
the brawl of storms cuffing window panes,
but a two-beat ballad, gentle as a shadow spring,
a mouse-pattering on the undergrowth.

Mushrooms have risen, tufts of grass on their caps
like the soft hats of cardinals. He plucks one, shaking
off spores, smoothes wetness from its head, smiles;
Close your eyes and open your mouth, he says.

CHAMBRE D'AMOUR

There's a moment at sunrise when morning has
a melon glow, and shutters sip pale cock-crow
light that sifts in rumours on marble floor;

your smell is a scarlet sound in my ears,
the taste of your freckles chimes in my throat,
endearments plane and curl in my mouth,

and I'm stirred to wake your body caked in sleep,
to lap my finger in the julep of your flesh,
bead my lips;

behind my eyelids, stop-lights fizz,
I soften into drowsiness once more.

Later, the notes of my naked soles on tile,
I spread the jalousies and afternoon falls in
like an eavesdropper, dressed to kill in summer's skin.

You yawn, stretch, your scent leans
towards me as you unsprawl from the sheet,
legs the rust of desert skies;

the misty dazzle of the fridge
ignites a silhouette around you.

Later still, when dusk has led away
the sun and treetops gargle stars,
and all that's left of twilight is the bite-marks

of birds, we exult in the coolness dribbling down
the moon-slit night, and I suck in the sherbet
of the sky until bubbles eat my tongue.

THE WOMAN WHO TALKS TO PLANTS

As if it makes a difference,
feeding dead letters of bark, like history,
to the Russian alphabet of brushwood, ivy, spent briar.
Lighting it, watching smoke unparcel, dizzy into air.

In the grass, the sound of a snake unsheathing itself
from the self it used to be.
*
In the before, before he left to be someone else, they built bonfires together,
frantic twigs that leapt to his spill, the fistful of sugar he threw.

And always, tomatoes, lusty from the vine, sweet gifts
to parted lips, filling each other with summer;
a blanket beside the embers.

Once, they watched two snakes entwining gracefully upwards,
a tenderness.
*
Now, in the after, friends bring wine and clichés, leave empty bottles.
She lines them by the sink from habit,
a row of pointing fingers.

In bed, the sheets huff up a sharp whiff of body she wishes were his.
Stiff as a bodkin, she resists the pull of the hollow,
feels him there even now, the secrets of his spine.

She often thinks of the snakes.
*
He's not coming back.
Autumn will fall again with its mould and mushrooms,
air scaled with ash, sunset rain like coppers from a pouch.
Her boots will break the backs of fallen leaves.

And still, there are times her tongue catches his kiss,
that last taste of green.
*
Wanton with promise, like flighty girls, the tomatoes
part from the vine without a second thought,
leaving empty shapes of themselves behind.

Soon, she'll dip her knife in iced water,
dice them, let go of summer.

BEYOND

This is the here and now the in-between
the sequel;
it's one step beyond the passion the put-asunder
the drowning by divorce,
when still you come up choking on tears and terror
and the never-ending
Why?
It's past the letting go letting it go
giving it away,
blessing all those anodyne men picked up
in pubs parks diners discos bars,
waiting-rooms of the discarded,
the kind of men who screen lust
with sympathy
to smoke you out,
men eager to offer a hand a bone
to help you let go, just a little,
honey,
before they move on, away
from your aching and the ache
in your wrist jaw
when their heads cock back, warding
off the moment, mouths wide in prayer
to mothers wives
God,
and your fraught vagina, the gift you let go,
their target jackpot goal for the night,
and washing relief into the soreness of it all
in every sordid hotel room

you've ever let go in,
too unloved to care, to take them
to the marriage bed where now you sleep alone
devoured by space;
and afterwards you watch your face in grimy panes,
haloed in the crying light of street lamps.
This is the here and now, the transit stop
between letting go and moving on.
The first step beyond.

SPACES

You just want to fill them, don't you?
Like Nature, abhorring a vacuum.
Once, the spaces of unused years
reached, or so it seemed, to infinity,
full of possibilities for filling them
and years to do it in.
You fleshed out your days with things
that seemed imperative,
left them behind as you
sped into your tomorrows.
You plugged the rifts between you with words
until you ran out of things to say,
and spaces ballooned in their place.

You can't fill what can't be filled.
You spread yourself thinly; it's
not enough, there are cracks, rents.
Now the spaces stretch no further
than a minute, an hour, a day hence.
What once was that field of stars
is empty now, though a filament
of sky-blue is sometimes visible.
Most of the time, there's nothing there.

A SUDDEN PLEASURE

A microphone fizzes; two nuns in anoraks
and ankle socks prepare to drone the *Ave*.
Backs stiffen, hands unpeg from pews;
the priest swings a funeral of smoke towards us.

There's no recipe for colour here, no
painted statues bar the Byzantine Christ, rays
of sun rising from his head like Medusa's snakes;
no frescoes, no stained glass relieve the blind grey,
only long legs of daylight reaching down
from roof panes, ghosting splendour
on an altar-cloth plain as farmhouse linen,
then moving to trace the coffin's inlay,
turn roses back to red.

A hop-scotch sound like mice in pipes;
a small collection of seconds and I pinpoint it, look up,
see a joyous burst of pigeons tap-dancing on the glass.

THE ITALIAN WAY

Standing at the bus-stop all tarted up for town,
we giggle at the gigolos peacocking up and down,
flashing cartoon-sparkles from pasta-sharpened teeth,
mega-galactic crosses from mats of sweaty fur,
ogling us with beady greed, wondering if we do,
touching the “bird”, make sure it hasn’t flown –
white patches on blue jeans;
cocky little mothers’ sons, pride of the working class,
make you cringe at thoughts of evening scrums, acid
armpits, fish-damp hands mauling the straps of your bra,
garlic clogging the hairs in your ears. Stuff that for a lark.

Probed by headlights, we turn away from dawdling cars
and lechery hurled like condoms from open windows
supposed to turn you on. Oh God! The Latin Lover,
so subtle, so suave! Wallies in a woodpile.
Two stop in a Merc, swap fancies, decide. *Ciao ragazze,*
volete un passaggio? A likely lift! We mutter nasties
with a supercilious glint to shiver their twinkle,
but they persist, throw us repartee and neon smiles;
we shrug, what the hell, let’s take the mickey;
they lick their lips and dribble cream.

They jolt us off to Brera where fat old hags tout contraband fags
and addicts flop in midnight corners; take us to Club Due,
hands sliding up our arms, wishing they were our thighs.
We suck at G and Ts, engaged in serious lies about our ages
and our livings; the boys lap it up, calculating, eager not to blow it.
On cue, the one says: *Spaghetti at my place?*

We exchange pained looks, here we go again, the gastronomic foreplay.
They will be peeved, poor sods!

A pram in the hall splits us with laughter; the one says sheepishly
it's his sister's and slams the bedroom door. Words hang in steam
as we wait for the water, eyes on the other as he whips up a sauce
to impress us. He closes in to kiss me, tall and serious
in the kitchen doorway; his beard reminds me of another time,
but it's too soon, I say, *You're barking up the wrong tree, buster!*
Tiger turns chicken, flippancy turns tail,
but later he tries again, exhumes memories ....

The beard's gone, the man's stayed,
and here I am in a foreign flat in a foreign land
wondering why my roots are tugging.

DEARLY BELOVED ....

It's a raw, deliquescent morning towards the end of May,
shredded-wheat clouds whip a sky of curds and whey
as we gingerly duck beneath Lord Nelson's fundamentals
into a spree of rain,

and sweep across the green, baring teeth and a flash
of saucy tongue at the ciné camera frisking
guests trooping to the church to pay homage or gloat,
or keen, like me.

There in the pale-mouthed porch he stands, polishing
his smile; he sees me, starts, spasm on the hook,
his longest-standing female friend (he'd still prefer me
on my back!).

He greets me, guying doom, eyes gushing new frontiers,
sighs as we hug, *Oh honey, you've come!* and clutches
my buttock in rapture – no overture by the bedroom door,
but a swift, swansong fondle.

Land-fat patriarchs juggle their change, bald pates pickled
in stained glass, eye the bloodshot silks and smirks
as relentless cobweb-ladies in lacy hats shed a lacy tear or two,
and I feel sick in my pew.

There's a flurry at the door, necks crane and creak in crescendo,
a polyhedral gasp burps like a damp squib,
the county crème congeal, begin to think in whispers,
the organ brays.

Grey-starched groom with face of jam twists a queasy grin
as he goosesteps to the altar, in perfect check; the bride wobbles
down the aisle in her Wonderbra, cream trifle-topping,
Queen to King Four.

You'll be mine in buttons and bows inwardly strains
as gnomic words chatter like reaper-blades, mowing
second thoughts and just impediments, and I sit
clutching my peace forever.

Murmurs skirmish in the air, the cathartic rite is over,
loose ends neatly knotted in the vestry; bags clasp in a chorus
of clicking as holy osculation seals their fate,
then everyone has a go.

They wade through mobs of machine-tooled smiles,
a concussion of cameras, colour-dragging rain;
Sposa bagnata, sposa fortunata – we pop to the pub
for a chaser.

WHAT DO YOU REMEMBER, GRANNY

A lot less at my time of life, dear, that's for sure.
They say your short-term memory goes first so you're left
with scraps, like negatives stuck at the back of a drawer.
When I do my remembering, it's the past that's clear
as a bell - misspent youth, my mother used to say -
so many places to go, things to do.
Like what? Rave-ups, sit-ins, concerts, marches,
exotic foreign films, pop music – Lucifer's tool
the oldies called it, as if their war wasn't -
mini-skirts, Carnaby Street, High Street Ken.
You won't remember Biba … Mary Quant? Is she still going?
Free love – what a stir that caused! Nothing like
the things they get up to these days, of course,
but you can hardly call it tame!
Those afternoons lying in the sun in Regent's Park;
I remember the grass was cool, sticky, almost wet.
I remember the exhilaration.
Look here, you can see it in our faces.
Oh yes, those boots were dead cool, emerald suede
from Anello and Davide and a bugger to keep clean.
Such extravagance for a girl on a grant.
Did you know they made those boots for The Beatles?
Goodness, where did that one come from? I *was*
a bit plump, not fat, exactly. Then I got thin again.
That bathroom floor, the lino was cold, sticky, almost wet.
I stood in the shower for ages, trying to get warm.
I remember the water turning pink,
sluicing down the plug hole, clockwise.

Who was it said you shouldn't make the same mistake twice?
Let that be a lesson to you.

MR WATT REALISES THE POTENTIAL

To the Distinguished Gentlemen of Glasgow University: Upon undertaking the repairs entrusted to me, it became apparent that Mr Newcomen's design creates excessive waste of time, steam and fuel when pumping water from flooded mines.
Your obedient servant, etc., etc.

While strolling on Glasgow Green one Sunday afternoon in May, I was struck by the idea of introducing a second chamber, separate from, but connected to, the main cylinder, with "steam jacket" insulation, thus ensuring more efficient use of energy, or "horse power", to use my own coinage, and economies on coal of nigh on seventy-five per cent. It was great good fortune that circumstances presented me with my new partner, Matthew Boulton, the affluent entrepreneur from Birmingham; and so, to that "city of a thousand trades", which promised much, despite Mrs Elton's gloomy observation. I staunchly opposed the notion of substituting high-pressure steam for low; indeed, so grave were my concerns that I vigorously petitioned the Government to outlaw such practice, citing the risk of explosions; my efforts were, regrettably, thwarted.

Most happily, a problem that dogged construction was cannily solved when John Wilkinson perfected precision-boring techniques for iron cylinders and snug-fitting pistons, though grievously, he later proved to be another knave who flouted my patents and built several engines himself, unbeknownst to me. The Courts found in my favour, but I had rather be fired from a cannon than press for moneys owed. My plans to transform reciprocating into rotary motion were stymied, albeit briefly, by James Pickard's patent on cranks, a hiccup I overcame by inventing the epicyclic sun and planet gear. My son, James, insists that, of all my inventions, parallel motion is the one I most prize, but in truth, I am proud of every one; never did I dream that my name would one day become a household word when, as a lad sitting in my mother's cottage, I first became fascinated with steam, watching it lift the lid of a boiling kettle.

FLYING HIGH

You must have read about us in the press,
we were splashed all over the tabloids
from Maine to Texas, some old photo
they conned from my worn-out mother
as she lay in a stupor on her ratty
old settee, brain sodden with moonshine.
The sheriffs tore at their hair
till there was hardly any left rooted,
but the poor loved us for being young, bold
and beautiful, the stuff of their wildest dreams.
We gave them the buzz of sex, drugs
and Rock 'n' Roll; no drugs or R 'n' R for us,
but the sex, well, it goes without saying.
It was the risk, the exhilaration
of foxing the law, like cheating death;
everything was heightened, sharp, sublime.
Sometimes we could barely wait
to get to camp before ripping
at each other's clothes, while the car
veered like a drunk between the trees.
Then suddenly, he turned fey, unhinged,
hatching outlandish plots,
tearing at the seams under the pressure,
staunching the cracks with hooch,
and I was treated like the little woman
whose opinions weren't worth a crap.
Our hold-ups became reckless, dangerous;
I stayed on because I loved him,
and who else did I have anyway?

When you ask me how I see my life,
I can only say those years with Cee
were exciting, a constant high;
I'd have preferred a happy ending -
after all, why rob banks for thousands
of dollars if you end up plugged full
of holes and six feet under
in a pauper's grave?

FISHING MANUAL

Select your bait with care,
a worm, a grub, an attractive morsel
of false modesty,
or, if circumstances require,
adopt a fly, hoist with false colours,
a traditional ploy;
Attach your chosen lure to the hook
of your compulsion,
check that it's secure
to foil
the under-swirl of social currents
and undesired predators;
Survey the waters you intend to invade,
ensure they're calm,
no swells, no backwash, no weirs,
preferably receptive, above all responsive;
Take a firm stance on solid ground,
feet slightly apart, poised,
and choose the perfect moment
to cast your line with its brilliant charms;
Angle your rod with the craftsmanship
of years,
consummate, streamlined, precision-tested,
and draw in your line,
not too gentle, not too rough;
Watch it unzip the water
as it comes towards you,
revealing the glorious, glossy splendour
of your catch:
The Compliment.

A DOG'S LIFE IN NEW YORK

Life in a mega-penthouse isn't always the money for jam
it's made out to be. Bunny, "I was born on Easter Day",
who owns the pad, has a menagerie.
This is all very well, but to my mind, four pillowy cats,
a spring-loaded hound and rugs on tiles spell bedlam,
plus the gilded-caged birds and the Olympic aquarium.
But that's Bunny for you.
The cats aren't so bad, they have their own litter-loos
where they scratch and hunch and pose like queens,
but Tobias Von Hollenstein III has to be taken to the park
four times a day, or Lord help the chair legs.
Not my cup of tea, coming from the Isle of Dogs like, but
it's one of the things I'm paid to do, so I crack on
with the stiff upper lip I brought over with me in steerage.
Walking Toby is less fraught since Bunny supplied
an extensible lead; no more fake strangulation-of-Toby scenes
every time we pass a tree, but he still gets this confused look
around the eyes when he's brought up sharp.

To be fair to the young mutt, he only tries to hare off
when he sees Princess Leila in the distance,
which is where she stays, being a princess.
He doesn't even get close, except at the parlour, where
they're strictly chaperoned and barricaded by toiletries.
He's lucky to have short hair and a groomer who's found
the G spot on his back end, but poor Leila's fleece takes ages
to blow and curl, and she's still gritting her teeth
as a ribbon is tied, just so, between her ears.
I suppose he thinks that sitting beside her among the brushes

and combs and hair-dryers gives him droit de seigneur,
but he's fated to pine from afar; he'll never be allowed
anywhere near her little outfits - plastic for rain, tartan for cold,
and the infernal ribbon in the colour du jour.
Come on young feller-me-lad, I say on his wishful-thinking days,
back to the zoo. He takes one last look over his shoulder, heaves
a sigh of longing, then trots along at heel with his tail held high.
Hard to match that for class, if I say so myself.

IF WISHES WERE HORSES

Sunday afternoon and I was mowing the lawn, working
off the Dog and Duck's Lunchtime Special.
She was knee-deep in foxgloves as I powered past, tiddly
from shandy and the rush of honeysuckle, not understanding
what I shouted over the motor, but grinning anyway.
I laughed at the cobwebs moored to her hair, her frantic flapping.

I'm not laughing now.
Here in the ICU, she's marooned on a bed that gets bigger
by the day, lifeless as a Butterick pattern.
Induced coma, they said. *Talk to her.*
So I do, as if the only thing separating us is the kitchen table
and I'm cussing *The Sun* while she tops-and-tails beans or shells peas.
Not about that afternoon though, not about the stone sheering
away from the blades, the blood, a bright terrible red running
to earth from her temple, her body folding like my old builder's rule.

Every afternoon the gals bring the tea trolley round.
Bun-or-biscuit, duck? one will say. *No, no beer! You are a card.*
I sip "the good Yorkshire brew", scalding my tongue again.
I often stare at that print on the wall opposite. When the sun shines
on it, I'd swear the wain edges forward; sometimes,
I wish I could jump into the hay and be carted away.
Sometimes, I drop off after the tea; when I wake up,
it takes me all my time to remember where I am.

I'm not one for praying, unless Forest is playing, but I've brought
one of her plaster angels because you never know, do you?
Her fingers will recognise it when she comes to;
I can't even contemplate "if".

NOT YET, NOT NOW

I'm going to do something today.
Not just any old thing, something big,
something I'll be remembered for,
noble even, like those slick words
stinking of curry tell my ear.

It was easy at first, intoxicating,
like a students' union, steamy nights,
passionate speeches, urgency;
it made me feel accepted, one of them.
They reeled me in gradually, slyly,
and before I knew it, I was in so deep
I couldn't get out. I don't know
if I even wanted to, even after
I'd cottoned on to their hidden agenda
and found I was on it. Truth be told,
I'd be a lost soul without them now,
all the brothers in the group would.

It was a mistake asking to see my mother -
poor woman, so PC, so blind, so *English.*
She was screaming and thrashing
when they dragged her out of the flat.
I was sorry about that, about calling her
an effing waste of space; she *is* my mother
after all, whatever she believes in.

They've synchronised the mobile phone,
buckled the holdall behind my back where

I can't get at it, and now I'm here,
walking down the steps of Euston Underground,
just another commuter in the rush-hour crowd.
And let me tell you something,
it may sound strange, but I'm not thinking
about infidels, or Allah's will, or Vestal Virgins,
all I'm thinking is *Not yet, not now.*

I give myself

a weekly treat: Friday nights, Il Vecchio Convento,
glad-eyed waitresses young enough to flirt with
(I'm no cloistered monk, thank the Lord).
Much as I'm beguiled by the beckoning
of prawns, the enticing anatomies
of mussels, it's the wine that's ceremonial.
Time was, I'd pour fire and brimstone down my throat.
These days, I'm old enough to discriminate.
I study the menu by the mystical glow of Barolo.

THE MISTRESS

Still as a cat at his voyeur's station,
he watches the Amstel running full-bosomed, and flesh,
at its beck, arranging and re-arranging itself.

It's his moment of genesis;
I catch his excitement like an expanding scent.

He calls to me in his river-wavy voice to fill his cup.
Today, I'm his pourer of wine; today, his muses
are the heron-like women on the bank.
I watch him study them, scrawling his graffiti-gaze
over figures lying like toppled statues of themselves,
the up-ended zed of a girl hugging her knees.

Don't for a minute think I'm jealous;
his passion for me is of a different ilk, endures
despite the worthy burghers shaking fists
and crying *Sin!,* crying *Whore!*

He mixes colours in a wild rush, splashes his smock
(the stains will stay no matter how hard I scrub.)
But see how he marries paint to canvas, magicking
the craquelure of waves breaking on the bias, lit from inside,
the bodies sprung from clown-bright frocks,
breasts swaying delight,
the Rembrandts of water and sky teasing nub and fold;
the blue surprise of a kingfisher lighting the shore.

AMON L'ISA

You don't know why I smile like this.
You with your modern jargon blame PMT
(as if it existed then),
and re-cast my pagan mysteries
with foxy adjectives like "enigmatic",
(great carbuncle of a word
for one so ... refined ... as I).

How things have changed since the old days.
Here I hang on my Louvre wall,
draped in complimentary light,
cosseted by humidity-controlled air,
all 31 by 21 inches of me,
smaller than many, larger than some,
greater than most.
What do you see, you Art tourists, when you look
at me with your faux-connoisseur gaze?
The smile for sure, so famous, dissected, discussed.
Behind my oily brush-strokes
I may be mocking your gullibility,
your eagerness to disbelieve your own eyes,
take common cant as gospel.
Tell me, do the double entendres and allusions
strike no chord at all?
Do you not note with satisfaction
some slight resemblance to my creator,
that Grand Master of the Priory?
Who, I must admit, was splitting his sides
at his little joke, it was a pleasure to watch.

But Leonardo, I said, being familiar by that time
and ravishing the “r”, “*they’ll never understand*
the trick with the horizon.”
He was laughing so much, the old rogue,
he forgot to paint in my eyebrows.

The Man who brought Copper and Gold

The sacred ring has emptied, but stone echoes within the stones and winds lend chorus to our coronach. He was my father, a shaper of metals, and passed to me the tarsal defect in his feet. This is the site where ancient solstice rites reside, where far-flung island tribes still flock to feast, to share their lore and ken. It's where he'll lie, many a crow's flight from his native Alps, in a wood-lined grave, knees bent, facing north; around him, tenfold the goods he'll need for his next life, signals of his trade and sway. In a land of flint and stone, the coppersmith was king.

THE PAINTER AND THE APPRENTICE

The table is a low trestle contraption cobbled together
by the family's odd job man in a fit of uncertain joinery.
It's a stark contrast to our stools, which are sturdy confections
with intriguing indents for the derrière, though the rims
cut into my overflowing buttocks like a penance.
I'm a Goliath beside him; some centimetres have been sawn
off the boy's stool, but still, his feet dangle below callipers
into empty space however much he wriggles;
I've suggested splints and bandages of ass's dung, but
the Filth Therapy cuts no ice in this progressive household.
My reluctance to take him on was a ruse, and brief;
my credit isn't what it was, but the tarnish
on my reputation hasn't yet winnowed its way
to the county aristocracy, and you have
to turn a *livre* where you can.
Yet Henri has an undeniable gift, and if you ignore
his legs, he's a pretty little morsel; his berry-red
pout already has me tossing in dreams.
We work so closely side by side that the innocent
grazing of his thigh against mine leaves me breathless,
his shoulder under the not-quite-avuncular brush
of my palm electrifies my jaded body.
I'm quick to grab a cloth when he tips a jar
and stains his britches with ochre, wiping off
the excess with meticulously slow strokes.
But I make a small error of judgement.
Appalled, I watch as bright red spurts from the back
of my hand, see the look in his eyes, defiant, aghast,
and in his fist, the canvas knife, drooling my blood.

THE LAST CATHARS AT CARCASSONNE

Depth in their cave is black as a pit,
no shine or shape;
it invites you to sink yourself down,
but offers no relief.

The floor is stone, not one, a sea,
each pressed against the next
to form a perfect reef
that gives no guarantees.

Sun is a word in a myth now,
moisture pinches where it falls
and always disappears
before your thirst is quenched.

There's no horizon, no signpost
measures how far life is from here,
and only muffled sounds tell you
something is happening outside.

They say

I'm old enough now to be told,
old enough to know about the bomb
they say
my parents died in the rubble,
buried under four storeys of concrete.
I was five months old; almost
every bone in my body was broken
they say
an English doctor mended me;
I'm lucky I only have scars, a limp
they say
afterwards, I was sent to a camp in Tunisia;
it took the doctor six months to trace me,
his miracle baby, spoke with a smile
of refugee quotas, Europe, England
they say
I can't go home, there's nothing left.
Maybe one day, one day
they say, they say

PAYBACK

It's a typical summer's day, a narcotic
kind of white with teenage menace
simmering in the 'hood. Today
he's getting even - an eye for an eye -
vowels slick as bullets.
He's had it with jeers and loser jokes
and today he's going to make
himself a hero.
He'll wait for them where
the railway arches peter
like serrated teeth to nothing,
which is what he'll blow them to
when they leave the lock-up.
He'll have women too when he's famous –
a diamond geezer with his personal gang
of fans getting off on adoration.
He'll even write a book.
He checks his shot-up ma has finally
ODed, and lets the pit bull loose
for when his pa staggers home.
He picks up the Kalashnikov
he got with his ma's methadone.
The barrel is smooth, tight, shiny,
like the burnt skin on his face.

THE HOUSE THAT SWALLOWED HER DOWN

Silence heals, but keeps a scar of terror her mind
snags on, thumb over knuckles,
after screams strip the house to brick,
walls skid into floor,
after hydraulics of his hard-on piston to standstill,
and he pulls his jeans to the jut of his belly,
re-loops the belt and leaves,
taking chaos with him like a dog on a lead.

She'll sit for a while, cowled in lamplight,
shuddering disfigurine in a paperweight,
thoughts unsynched like first raindrops,
memories skating into one another.

When her thighs stop colliding, she'll wipe tears
and snot, shadows sliding down her legs;
she'll clean the tooth she finds in a pool,
put it in the box with others.

Somehow, she'll go on.
She'll paint her eyelids painful blue.
She'll seal her lips with Cherry Red.
She'll accept the flowers/chocolates/pleas.
She'll wait for the next time the smiling man
who did this comes home, body cycling on alcohol,
hands full of themselves.

HAMARTIA

Behind the bedroom door,
flattened carpet the same shape
as your Minnie Mouse slippers.
You listen for the creak of wooden stairs,
his feet finding their evening echoes.
He isn't coming. You know he will.
You know his smell. It fills your throat.
You won't cringe, you're not a beaten dog. You do.
Someone must hear. Your mother won't.
She's got new ear plugs for her iPad.
You'd kick and scratch, draw her blood,
if she hadn't bled enough already.
Your sister hears.
I'm too old for him. Not old enough to stop him.
Yesterday, I killed the smug silence
of the door hinge with a hammer. It keens.
You try to hide. He knows all your secret places.
He won't find this one. He always does.
You can shut your eyes tight as a hug,
it won't make you invisible.
It's not his fault. It's a special love.
You don't know any better.
Your father rapes you. He doesn't.
The rasp-pink of his face gives him away.
Threads of glass are twined so tight inside you
you know they're going to snap.
Everything shatters. Walls are red. They're blank.
Your eyes are huge, pale, the eyes of a beggar.
He kills you. You haven't died.

Minutes are a rosary. Minutes are just time passing by.
The room settles. It's white again. It never was red.
He runs his voice over your name like a brook.
He makes promises. He won't keep them.
Makes you promise not to tell. You haven't.
Later, your sister will come and hold you close,
as if it might protect you from tomorrow.
I'll slip into the bed and fit around you
like a whispered conversation, a fairy-tale,
a happy ending.
When the door is silent.

ACT OF MERCY

She makes vague rustling sounds at the back
of her throat, as if a mouse is nesting there.
He lifts her head, careful not to catch thistles of hair.
It's strangely comforting to press his face
into the pillow, breathe in what's left of her.
He remembers to put on latex gloves.
It doesn't take long.
Afterwards, he lies beside her on the bed,
and, finally, sleeps.

OVER THE LINE

The phone call comes out of the blue, a voice
sizzling with hysteria; it makes my stomach lurch.
She insists on Soho, miles from where she lives,
a wine bar where you can lose yourself in crowds.

She sways on the threshold, bumped by people
entering, leaving, thin as a reed, purple shadows
under her eyes like paint on enamel,
blonde hair lank, not washed in days.

She sits down with a sigh too big for her size,
clutching her bag as if something precious is inside.
She unwinds her scarf slowly; it's like watching her
undress, or bare grief, I can't tear my eyes away.

I see them then: twin pansies beside her wind-pipe.
He wanted to do something no one had ever done to me before.
She hands me an envelope; it's crumpled, stained.
If anything happens to me, tell the Police I wasn't mad.

And she's gone. Her scarf has slid to the floor,
unnoticed; I stare at it, the paisley pear shapes;
it looks like a rickle of tears,
but perhaps they're my own.

WHEN THEY SAID I HAD IT COMING

my insides did cartwheels,
my tongue tasted bile,

pork scratchings and printer's ink,
gravel pits and Jurassic cliffs, killer carp,
the floating pub at Castle Wharf, sugar beet, heron,
the long-distance lope of the Fosse Way
and my weary mother, chicken feathers in her hair,
the old pit and its slag heaps and sirens, the dust it rained
on Granddad's rhubarb and miners' claggy coughs,
raves in abandoned factories and ladies free on Fridays,
punks on fast burn and lock up your daughters,
necking bottles of whatever and Mickey Finns
and dog ends crushed in cans,
and the 67 bus to Northgate,
and Liz and Kath and me on the lash,
brazen legs, tank tops and sequins
and Kath's dragon tattoo coming unstuck,
and hoodied gangs self-seeding in despair, sleazy malls
and living rough, the grim multi-storey
and the chap who threw himself off,
a trillion stars and floating on the Milky Way
and hands I didn't know on my skin
and purple hieroglyphs,
my new skirt ripped, one white sling-back lost,
and drool on my face and sweat and *something*,
and someone stopping up my mouth,

and when they found me, the girls said *Did you pull?*
but the words I wanted to say I'd swallowed whole.

STOCKHOLM SYNDROME

He's stolen someone else's voice;
it's low and mellow at the edges,
a thickness wrapped around the vowels,
a buried sound.
His fingers press white
into her nape where it's tender,
wind tight into her hair,
arching her spine backwards.
In the light from the naked bulb
her hands send shadows
onto the wall, settle like fledgelings on his.
She's learnt not to kick
and scratch – it got her nothing
but cuts and bruises and days
tied up on a skanky mattress.
Better to pander to his vanity,
bolster his self-esteem,
make him like her.
He's already let her take off
his mask and sooner or later,
he'll stop chaining her when he leaves.
Eventually, he'll bring her up from the basement
to a kind of freedom.
Then she'll decide whether to make
a run for it, or stay, as she swore
she would when she was pleading.
Maybe she will stay, she's getting
hooked, addicted to him.
The magic of close quarters.

Not to mention the small matter
of the ransom money,
another kind of freedom.

BATHERS

The first sound to reach him was laughter.
Stock still in his leafy hide, he spied on
the women flitting through the copse - five
or six, he couldn't be sure - down the sloping bank
to the river, unloosing parachutes
of dandelion clocks, detonations of grass seeds.
He watched as they untied bonnets,
shaking out curls, unlacing corsets
with soft grunts and sighs, giggles,
backs curving to unhook boots.

He closed his eyes, and when he opened them again,
there was the tableau: the boldest girl had splashed
into the river, flung her chemise to the shore,
squealing as the waves she made came back to spank her.
Others dipped their buttocks first, conch-shell hands
ladling water to breasts, arms, necks,
giddy with abandon.

They never knew he was in the trees,
wouldn't have known his name,
wouldn't have recognised themselves
in the abstract figures he painted from memory.

THE SMUG AND SILVER TRENT

Thirty species of fish once
Who fishes it now?
Locals do. Lads do.
Sly waters that make them reckless.

Mercia Mudstones, red strata
They drag tackle, net, pail, stopping
at an inlet sleek with gravel.
A rusty kitchen chair waves an arm
on its way to the gannet's bath.

Triassic Sherwood sandstones
Flies glint. Lines sail. They hurl and haul,
jeering at hooked boots, jellied condoms.
Mud sucks their waders with every step.

Jurassic limestone, Lincolnshire Edge
One boy lost his footing, jerked by the sudden tug
on his rod. They all remember
the yelling, the echo of splashing feet

Aquifers, marls, Aegir
as the man charges into the water,
bubbles slicking off him as he lifts
the spluttering child: *never, ever, ever ...*

THE CUTTER

He loves me, he loves me not ...
Petals pulled from daisies
give random answers; dandelion puffs
carry wishes too far and wide.
There are no daisies here, no dandelions,
only the blithe tiles of a bathroom,
the loop of minutes,
lurch of time.
Sweat inches down her midriff,
a liquid sword, stops dead
at the waistband of her shorts.
It distracts her.
She looks in the mirror, surprised
to meet herself there.
Will she? Won't she?
Breathe in, breathe out; spiked heartbeats.
Her glass-twin is fraying at the edges:
Will you make your mind up?
She hears a mountain falling
in her head, a jangle of voices not
her own: *She who hesitates...*
No, take a deep breath, hold it in ...
Close your eyes, don't look ...
Remember you'll be one of us ...
Pinch your thigh, that's right ...
The razor-blade glints
silver,
red.

EGO TRIP

You know this woman,
you've seen her replicants countless times.
She glides hotfoot from her steam-less, stainless kitchen,
wearing the shield of her starched apron,
her helmet of starched hair,
and from behind the Botox, the expert matt of her YSL,
the expert feathering of her eyebrows, smoky-black liner,
she exclaims: *God! What a fright I must look!*
Not at all, you say, *lovely as ever* as her expert gaze
levies confirmation like a pre-prandial toll,
then lights on your man.

Or,
she poses in the gold from the fire,
backed by the complicity of candles,
artfully abandons her sherry on the mantelpiece
with a gesture designed to draw eyes,
runs her hands over the hungry-red silk of her hips,
and stage-sighs: *The shop girl swore this colour*
was perfect for my complexion, but, I don't know,
perhaps it makes me look just a teeny bit sallow?
You mumble something vague;
it doesn't really matter what you say,
sometimes the right sound is enough,
because her focus is on the desired effect
as it leers towards her.

Such a fragile thing, the ego: tap it at the fontanel
and it'll crack and spill.

Yet how resilient: batter it with adverts
and new looks and it'll swell,
forging fresh paths of self-interest,
like bindweed.

OBVIOUS

It was obvious from the start, plain
as the nose on Billy Smith's face, great
candle snuffer of a thing with a drip forever
dangling over his Mexican moustache.
It was clear as day to anyone with eyes
and an ounce of sense –
the Mauds, Mays and Ethels for example,
who had eyes in the back of their heads
and tongues like cleavers.
And her, the village bike, with her halter necks
and jealous red hair, slinking her body
round the juke-box under the nose
of every Tom, Dick and Harry,
and poor Billy thinking he was the only one
when it was obvious he wasn't.
Then she got knocked up and that
was obvious too, even to Billy. And when
he hanged himself from the rafters in his barn,
the tribe of Toms, Dicks and Harrys tugged
jug ears, tweaked Aertex vests, twanged braces.
And the Mauds, Mays and Ethels clucked,
smoothed feathers, underpinned their bosoms
with a nowt-to-do-with-me crossing of arms.
They all said *that* hadn't been on the cards
and it just went to show that where there's no sense
there's sometimes feeling, but everybody knew,
didn't they,
that someone born with a hooter like that
was bound to be unhinged.
It was obvious.

THE PEACH GROWER'S LAST REQUEST

They said he was a cross-grained man, all prune
and prism, face like the bark of the trees he nursed;
said he was born with a kink and pity his wife,
poor lamb, who found out the hard way and hid
his shotgun when the blue devils struck;
said best not to think of the touch of cold steel,
better to find compassion and forgive.

What no one could forget was the note he'd propped
against the *moca* machine. He'd put no signature,
just the spidery words: *Don't go into the bathroom.*

HAND AT HIGH TIDE

A tarred line on the pile signals high tide;
above it, a number carved in feet and inches.
The measurement is an end in itself,
important only as a marker; it has no bearing
on flux, no bearing, when tides swell to full,
on the hand wearing a bracelet of weed, waving
in the lurch and buck around the pier, sinking
as waters ebb to join the body shuttered
in darkness, tethered by algae,
and a chain.

The vixen

thinks she's safer close to town, doesn't know
about the crones in shawls and clogs, secrets
tucked in pinafore pockets, smug as grenades.
Eventually, these matrons will stumble on ruffs
of bloody quills, a half-hen left for later,
and men with guns and dogs will stomp through
the wood, lifting tiny kites of brown and green.

In the light-burst from my torch, her eyes
are holes in autumn leaves; I whisper my *bewares*
into a night that's slick with silence now.

THUNDERBOLT

A great elm stood on the cape, closer each year
to the edge as the cliff nibbled inland. It was a landmark
in these parts, a monument to Nature surviving
against the odds. I expected every winter to be its last,
but come spring, it always proved me wrong.

That evening, I stood beneath its dislocated
joints, grinning as seals at play scarved themselves
in spume. It was that magical, downy hour just
before dusk when you can almost believe in sprites.

The wind rose out of the blue; no matter, I was used
to sudden squalls and normally turned back in time.
But I was mesmerised; it was like watching a god launch
tins of indigo, purple, black to curdle sunset.
The storm roiled landward, and still I didn't move.
Instead, I leaned into the wind in ecstasy, arms
spread wide, face upturned like a pagan worshipper,
lit by dragon-tongues of lightning.

They say the last thing you see is imprinted forever
on your retinae; I looked up through the shattering
boughs at the explosion of light, and blinked, once.

There, on the old Salt Route

stiff-kneed on a granite slab
in a disused chapel,
chill gnawing on a draught,
light plucking at the gloom.
The air's heavy with the must and rot
of long-ago flowers, incense,
the sad, sweet smell of dusty pastry.
Christ looks down
from His Last Supper
over a row of disfigured candles,
charred matchsticks;
his disciples break bread,
smudges in the dusk like the pattern
of wallpaper through paint.

The story pauses here, balanced
on one foot as it were.
Then, the altar lamp flares
in its spider's net,
a convulsion
of new light, new shade,
Christ glinting now with crushed
jewels in tempera, gazing benignly
(or is it sadly?), not at crusts,
but a feast, symbols - cheese,
meat, fish, ruby wine -
an oddly knowing gaze, totting up
the balance-sheet of mankind.
And comes the thought:
how cold this chamber,
this forgotten chapel.

UPLAND CASTRUM

Seen in shade from far away, it's a hand-print inked
on the hillside, fingers splayed to crenellate the sky;
up close, its walls are the crumbling paradigms
of a fossilised tongue, stones consoled by lichen,
a skelter of nettles, wild orchids spilling pearls.

Now, crows mimic the cries of merchants once
grown fat on trade with China, ladies' soft gossip
is the wing-swoop of kites, the flittering of bats
in the spidery damp where urchins used to play.

Someone, a traveller offered lodging, or a transient
squatter perhaps, has nailed to the castle gate a clock
that's lost its hands, and below it, Swiss-knifed
in the oak is an arrowed heart encircling

Franco ama Maria
per sempre

SILVER

(A found poem)

Silverback	an alpha male mountain gorilla with silvered hair across its back.
Silver bullet	the only weapon believed capable of killing a werewolf.
Silver fern	*Cyathea dealbata,* or *punga* in Maori, a tree fern found in New Zealand forests, a stylised national emblem.
Silverside	the upper, choicer part of a round of beef.
Silver-stick	a field officer of the Life Guards attending the sovereign on state occasions, carrying a silver rod.
Silverweed	*Potentilla anserina,* a small grassland shrub, with yellow flowers, silvery compound leaves and herbal properties.
Silver	Objects capable of bonding.

WISTERIA LANE

Nellie Hayes pushed herself through the crowd –
easy enough when you're built like a JCB.
She was beside herself, pink from chest to cheek,
almost popping from her pinny, spluttering tales
of men in Black Marias and screeching tyres.
Ivy Jones said she was kneeling in darkness, peeping
round her lace curtains when the shenanigans began.
She phoned Madge next door, met her by the gate
under the false acacia to watch the goings-on.
Old Joe Brown was in his porch, but didn't notice
anything what with his cataracts, bless him, until
the arc lights came on and by then it was all over.
No, he wasn't here now, he was at home consoling
himself with a meals-on-wheels biriani and a pint
of stout and was unavailable for comment.
Local trophy wives, the callipygian Poppy Van Ackers
and Marigold Tanner, almost swooned as SWAT teams
poured over the pavement like, quote, "ink on milk".
Lucky for both that their husbands were on hand to ply
them with well-chilled Prosecco and low-cal crisps.
Young Johnny Bragg got as far as saying it was a load
of old ** before his dad gave him a clout round the head.
Neighbourhood nerds said they were reconstructing
the scene on blogs, but as they'd been busy hacking
during the raid, it would be more fantasy than fact.
The Seymours and Silvers said their dogs had been
utterly terrified by the noise of shots, dustbins crashing,
yells that sounded like *Drop your weapon, On your knees,*
Hands behind your head, but there'd been one hell of a din,
so couldn't be absolutely sure.

The men in shiny suits and Hushpuppies sucked their teeth and pens, hard put to assess facts (for the broadsheets) and fiction (for the tabloids), since no eye-witness story tallied with another. But on one thing they all agreed: Tom Cruise was a lot shorter than they'd thought.

TEA AND BISCUITS

Tea or wine? he says, and winks.
It's mid-afternoon. *Tea then*, pouring himself Merlot.
He offers chocolate fingers. Another wink.
One too many.

It's theatre, a peacock's tail, a manakin's moon dance
of heady bouquets, all colour and lust,
clinches to tip the pedal-point of passion; then,
distance, brisk, deliberate: *Let's get your laptop sorted.*

And always, *How did you* do *that?,* his sleight
of hand juggling synch, status, up-grades,
pop-up windows, configurations
too swift to follow.

He slouches by the sink now, foxy glint in his eye.
She forgets how tall he is till he backs her against the fridge,
keeps her captive with his Cadbury tongue.
Water rouses in the kettle for tea she'll let grow cold.

They sit thigh-close on the sofa, mug and glass
colluding on the coffee table.
One of them reaches for the biscuits, keeps one,
gives one, like lighting two cigarettes.

She watches him through mites of dust in a sunbeam,
tempted to lick away a smear on his lip. Instead,
squeezes the muscle above his knee, makes him jump;
she can't tell from his skin if he's blushing.

One of them points to the white mayhem
in the orchard: *There'll soon be cherries.*
She smells the raw edge of spring on his neck;
bright spots light on her cheeks, like little songs.

When the biscuits are gone, one of them will call it a day.
They'll hug goodbye, a swaying au revoir, dance-floor smooch.
Their smiles will be enigmatic, give nothing away.
One of them will say: *I'll ring you.*

Holding Hands at their Age

Grasses whisker dunes that roll away like double chins;
Harry points from a ridge like a jack tar sighting land,
lists seawards with the weight of the hamper,
kicking riffs of sand from his heels.
Maud, in a billow of pink, tethers herself to his shadow,
cursing under her breath at each twinge of her bunions.

Harry wrestles the deckchairs, peeks to see if she's watching.
What if mine collapses? thinks Maud, biting her lip
as she pictures herself in a marshmallow heap, frock
round her neck, airing her promise.
She pats her frizzing perm, ties knots in a hankie,
twirls it till it belly-flops. She could murder a cuppa.

He roots in the hamper for yesterday's *Mail*,
retreats behind the sports page humming the Man U theme.
The warm brown tang of seaweed tarries in his nostrils:
memories, courting on Southend pier, grinning
from cartoon cut-outs, Maud's ankles, slimmer then,
as he prised her stiletto from a gap in the planks.

She's gripped by the urge to kick up her heels, fling off the traces,
tugs at her pop-socks with a defiant flourish, laughing out loud
at the leer on his face. Harry smirks, puppets cooped-up toes
in his socks; he rolls one off stripper-style, throws it, like a blown kiss,
to Maud who frowns at the spindly white shin gasping at the light,
wondering for the umpteenth time where all the hair has gone.

TAYARRA, THE RACING CAMEL

(late 1980s, Saudi Arabia)

It's almost time:
she sniffs the change in the air, day cooling to dusk,
yanks her tether in mischief,
flicks her tail at fat and fecund flies.

It's time:
she nuzzles the boy when he comes, sharing breath
as he rests his cheek on her muzzle
where the skin's soft as apricot,
calming her to kneel for the satin saddle
behind her hump, the straps Velcroed
round her belly, his legs on her ribs.

She jerks upright, steps to the mark,
all muscle and bone, haunches like Scottish hills.
Butterflies fidget in her stomach
as she waits for the starter's shout,
the down-swipe of his stick.
When it comes, she bursts from the line,
sand nipping at her hooves,
a collage of open mouths in the stands.

The boy hangs on for dear life, buttocks
thudding to her rhythm, wind gibberish
in his ears, chanting his mantra.
She doesn't need his prayer or the switch in the air;

she's a camel with speed in her blood,
a legend in the making.

Those who remember still say she ran for joy.

RANA ARBOREA

You can just make him out -
his shape, his dorsal skin almost
a precious stone, smooth, bright.
He sits quietly puffing out
his small breaths at the edge
of the pond by the willows.

He's caught in a spire of light
from a moon sagging to full –
trees become ink stains,
cobwebs etched on black,
each flower stalk long-necked
and sharp – until movement
breaks the surface of the water,
a trout heaves up, stealing silver,
and the frog jumps back
into just another leaf.

CIRCUS ELEPHANT GOES AWOL

It's a quirk of fate that, as George Sanger's wife
(*nom de cirque* Pauline de Vere) is reincarnating herself
as Britannia for the parade in her gilded ten-ton carriage,
'Lord' George's star turn, Charlie, is revelling
in the smells of Watney Street market
and remembering Africa;
that, as Mme S. (a splendiferous figurehead) flies
off the handle because her pachyderm is missing,
Charlie's plundering the costermongers' barrows,
which is when he gets wind of the boy - let's imagine
it's Johnny Swallow, future trainer of elephants -
who's dreaming his way past stalls and back-pedalling crowds,
and the only sound is a collective drawn breath
as he wraps his trunk around Johnny's waist
and hoists him aloft as if he were George S. Junior,
so that Johnny finds himself swinging up
to the top of the world, not knowing whether to laugh
or cry, and trying to hold on to his porridge.

SECRET LIFE OF A WINE CELLAR

Call me heartless if you will,
but there was no love lost between us.
He may be a lonely old Bavarian now,
festering in a corner where the bricks are damp,
but there was a time, before his cronies were taken,
when his gang lorded it here, sparkling with arrogance.
Look at him now, a fusty has-been with a bad temper
and a flavour like licking tin.

Give me young bloods every time, they stir things up,
add zest with their metallic chatter and saucy capers.
Close to me now is a coterie of pretty French minxes,
coquettes the lot, so pinkly fresh and impudent,
jiggling with youth and vigour,
they'd do the can-can if they could.
Sometimes it's a carnival in here; I hear them
giggling with the frisky young swains
from Sicily that cavort and serenade,
and every so often, a roué flutter ruffles
my depths, and I'm tempted to join in.
But maturity will out - after all, I'm now
a venerable Italian gentleman of impeccable DOC
and have my dignity to maintain.
Still, when the moon's full, I'm stirred
to dally, to seduce with my crimson scent,
and, *Mamma mia*! if I were twenty years younger
I'd give those fillies a run for their money!

SCHOOLGIRLS' ONE-TO-TEN DATING GUIDE

Our faces are busy with shadows
in the undecided light of cigarette smoke.
Ten-decks disappear with a snap of knicker elastic.
They fill their lungs and turn to me.
I know I'm snookered.

How far d'you let him go, then?
leaning against the sloppy stitching of moss
on the trunks of oaks, smiling the sly smile
of girls who know more than they should.
I lie and say Number Five.

They rub at vaguely Pansticked love-bites.
Di'n't think you'd get past Three.
My mouth opens to confess I'd bolted at the first
hint of French, hands that weren't mine,
the falling somewhere inside me.

Instead, I say he wasn't a good kisser, as if
I'd ever kissed more than the back of my hand,
the wardrobe mirror or posters of pop stars.
They look me up and down till I feel ugly.
You'll never get a fella like that.

A Swiss knife appears from nowhere,
gouges hearts and arrows,
wonky initials of Sutton's bad boys.
Trick is tactics, yeah? Your game plan.
Your One to Ten

A snigger. Flick of hair.
Setting out technicolour details with gusto.
Fear and something I can’t yet name
swill together in my stomach.
I gasp at the grossness of ‘going all the way’,

sure I’d never do anything as filthy as that,
until one day, I did.

www.ingramcontent.com/pod-product-compliance
Lightning Source LLC
Chambersburg PA
CBHW062112160726
48282CB00026B/770
* 9 7 8 9 3 8 8 3 1 9 5 9 1 *